Bond

C000215862

Maths

10 Minute Tests

10–11+ years

Andrew Baines

OXFORD
UNIVERSITY PRESS

1

What fraction of 2 hours is 15 minutes?
Circle the answer.

$\frac{1}{4}$ $\frac{1}{2}$ $\frac{2}{15}$ $\left(\frac{1}{8}\right)$ $\frac{1}{3}$ ✓

2

A 24-hour digital clock shows:

21:42

What would the time be if it were shown
on a 12-hour clock?
Circle the answer.

A 9.42   **B** 9.42 am   **C** 9.42 pm

D 12.42 pm   **E** 8.42 pm

3

What are the coordinates of Q?
Circle the answer.

A (0.7, 0.9)   **B** (0.9, 0.7)   **C** (1.9, 0.7)

D (1.7, 0.9)   **E** (0.5, 0.6)   ✓

4

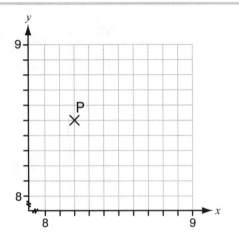

Using the grid, write down the coordinates
of P.

(8,2, 8.5)   ✓

5

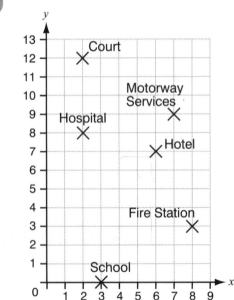

Where is the hotel?

(6,7)   ✓

6

Give the coordinates of the train station.

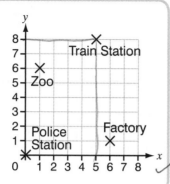

(_5_ , _8_)

7

Which of the following options correctly lists the coordinates of all three points?

Circle the answer.

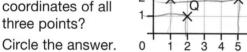

A P(1, 2)   Q(2, 1)   R(5, 2)

B P(2, 1)   Q(1, 2)   R(2, 5)

C P(1, 2)   Q(1, 2)   R(5, 2)

D P(2, 1)   Q(2, 1)   R(5, 2)

E P(1, 2)   Q(2, 1)   R(2, 5)

✓

8

What are the coordinates of the points R, S and T?

Circle the answer.

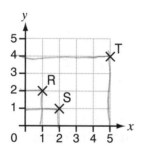

A R(1, 2)   S(2, 1)   T(4, 5)

B R(2, 1)   S(1, 2)   T(4, 5)

C R(1, 2)   S(2, 1)   T(5, 4)

D R(1, 1)   S(2, 1)   T(4, 5)

E R(1, 2)   S(1, 2)   T(5, 4)

✓

9

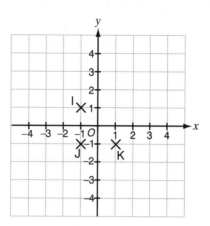

What are the coordinates of the points I, J and K?

Circle the answer.

A I(−1, 1)   J(1, 1)   K(1, −1)

B I(1, −1)   J(−1, −1)   K(−1, 1)

C I(−1, 1)   J(−1, −1)   K(−1, 1)

D I(1, −1)   J(−1, −1)   K(1, −1)

E I(−1, 1)   J(−1, −1)   K(1, −1)

✗

10

A, B and D form three corners of a square.

What are the coordinates of point C, which completes the square?

Circle the answer.

(2, −2)   (−2, 2)   (−2, −2)   (2, 2)   (2, 0)

✓

Total 8½

/10

TEST 2: Number

 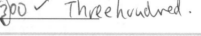

1   What is the number 59 038 in words?
Circle the answer.

(A) Fifty-nine thousand and thirty-eight ✓

B   Five hundred and ninety thousand and thirty-eight

C   Fifty-nine thousand three hundred and eighty

D   Five thousand nine hundred and thirty-eight

E   Five hundred and nine thousand and thirty-eight

2   Ninety thousand nine hundred and nine.
Which answer shows this written as a number?
Circle the answer.

99 099   99 999   (90 909) ✓
90 009   90 099

3   103 247
The 2 in this number is worth two hundred.
What is the three worth?
Circle the answer.

A   Three hundred   **B**   Thirty
C   Three   **D**   Thirty thousand
(E) Three thousand   ✓

4

Find a number for the blank space so that the list is in order of size.
2.35, 2.39, ..., 2.42
Circle the answer.

(A) 2.40 ✓   **B**   2.3   **C**   2.421
D   2.381   **E**   2.30

5

13, 130, ..., 13 000, 130 000
What should be the value of the 3 in the missing term?

1300 ✓   Three hundred.   ½

6   From the list find the smallest number.
Circle the answer.

7.6   7.06   7.60   (7.006)   7.600   ✓

7

In a class of 30 pupils, 11 are girls.
Approximately what proportion are boys?
Circle the most appropriate answer.

$\frac{1}{2}$ $\frac{11}{30}$ $\frac{1}{3}$ $\left(\frac{2}{3}\right)$ $\frac{5}{6}$ ✓

8

To make 2500 ml of orange squash, 500 ml of concentrate must be used.
What proportion of water must be used to make up the rest?
Circle the answer.

$\frac{1}{5}$ $\frac{1}{4}$ $\left(\frac{4}{5}\right)$ $\frac{3}{4}$ $\frac{2}{5}$ ✓

9   7.6324
What is this number to two decimal places?
7.63   ✓

10   8.9956
What is this number to two decimal places?
Circle the answer.

9.00   (8.99)   8.90   9.0000   9.0056   ✗

Total 8½

Test time: 0 .... 5 .... 10 minutes

1

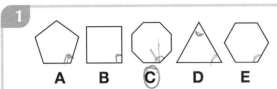

A   **B**   **C**   **D**   **E**

An angle inside a polygon is called an interior angle.

Which of the above polygons has the smallest interior angle?

Circle the answer.

D ✗

2

Which of the following shapes has nine diagonals?

Circle the answer.

A Pentagon   **B** Quadrilateral   **C** Octagon

D Triangle   **E** Hexagon

E ✗

3

Which of these makes a word when rotated through 180°?

Circle the answer.

SIH   ISH   HIS   SHI   IHS ✓

ITIS

4

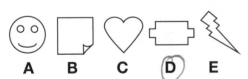

A   **B**   **C**   **D**   **E**

Which of these shapes has rotational symmetry?

Circle the answer. ✓

5

Which of these does not have a vertical line of symmetry?

Circle the answer.

MUM   TAT   HAH   LAL   XOX ✓

6

Which of these has a horizontal line of symmetry?

Circle the answer.

DID   CAT   HUH   NUN   TAT   ✗

7-8

What is the perimeter of each of the shapes below?

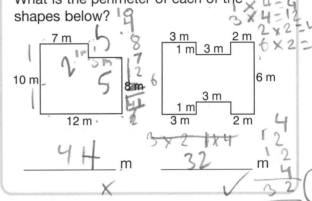

_44_ m ✗

_32_ m ✓

9

Which shape has a different perimeter from the others?

_D_ ✓

10

What is the perimeter of this shape?

Circle the answer.

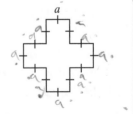

A $12a$ **B** a^{12} **C** $6a$

D $aaaaaa$ **E** a^6

A ✗

Total 5

1

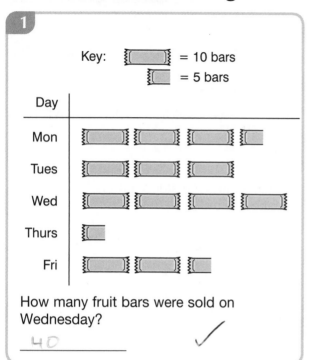

Key: = 10 bars
= 5 bars

Day	
Mon	
Tues	
Wed	
Thurs	
Fri	

How many fruit bars were sold on Wednesday?

40 ✓

2

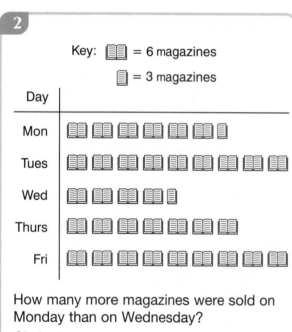

Key: = 6 magazines
= 3 magazines

Day	
Mon	
Tues	
Wed	
Thurs	
Fri	

How many more magazines were sold on Monday than on Wednesday?
Circle the answer.

A 12 ✓   **B** Can't tell   **C** 2
D $6\frac{1}{2}$ **E** 0

3

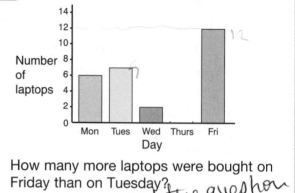

How many more laptops were bought on Friday than on Tuesday? *read the question.*
pay attention ✗

7

4

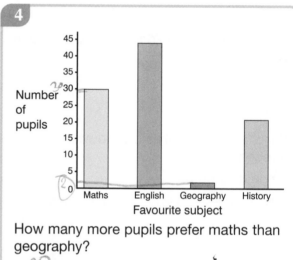

How many more pupils prefer maths than geography?

28 ✓

5

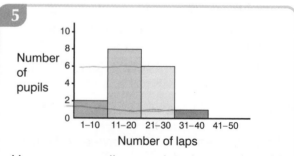

How many pupils completed more than 20 laps in a charity race? ✓

7

6

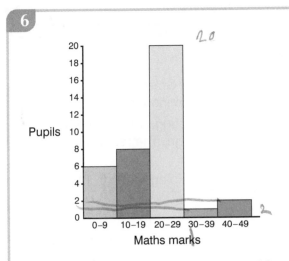

20

2

Maths marks

The pass mark for a maths test was 20.
How many pupils passed the test?

_____23_____ ✓

---

7 bag = 12.

A bag contains 2 red, 4 green and 6 yellow marbles. Lily picks a marble at random.

In which of the options below are both statements true? Circle the answer.

A You have an even chance of picking a yellow marble.
You have a greater than even chance of picking a red marble. ✗

(B) You are certain to pick a marble.
You have a greater than even chance of picking a yellow marble.

C You have a less than even chance of picking a red marble.
You have a less than even chance of picking a green marble.

D You have a greater than even chance of picking a yellow marble.
You have a less than even chance of picking a green marble.

E You have a greater than even chance of picking a green marble.
You have an even chance of picking a yellow marble.

8

Jo rolls a fair dice numbered 1 to 6. In which of the options below are both statements true?
Circle the answer.

A You have an even chance of rolling an even number.
You are certain to roll a number less than six.

B You have an even chance of rolling a prime number.
You are certain to roll a number less than seven.

C You have a less than even chance of rolling an odd number.
You are certain to roll a number less than seven.

D You have a greater than even chance of rolling a prime number.
You are certain to roll a number less than five.

(E) You have a less than even chance of rolling a prime number.
You have an even chance of rolling an odd number. ✗

9

A bag contains some coloured balls.

There are: 3 black, 2 red, 5 blue, 6 green and 7 yellow.

Ranjna picks a ball at random.

What is the chance that she doesn't pick a red ball?

_____2/21_____ 2 out of 21 ✗ $\frac{21}{23}$

10

When Eric spins the spinner, what is the probability that it will land on a number greater than 1?

3 out of 4 $\frac{3}{4}$ ✓

6

Total

1   1   8   9   (15)   16

Look at these numbers. Which is neither a square number nor a cube number?

Circle the answer.   ✓

2   (1)   2   9   (16)   25

Look at these numbers. Which is both a square number and a cube number?

Circle the answer.   ✗

3

Which option shows two prime numbers that add up to make a cube number?

Circle the letter.

(A) 3 and 5 ✓   **B** 1 and 7   **C** 2 and 6

D 5 and 120   **E** 4 and 12

4

Look at the pattern below:

Line 1   1 = 1

Line 2   1 + 3 = 4

Line 3   1 + 3 + 5 = 9

Line 4   1 + 3 + 5 + 7 = 16

Line 5   1 + 3 + 5 + 7 + 9 = 25

Line 6   1 + 3 + 5 + 7 + 9 + 11 = 36

How many prime numbers would line 6 contain?

___3___ 4

5

Out of 567 people surveyed, 78 preferred curries, 206 preferred stir-fries and the rest preferred pasta.

How many liked pasta?

___183___

3̶5̶6̶ 7
284
1̶8̶3̶   ✗

6

127 children from Grassmoor Primary School are performing a show.

72 children are acting, 49 children are assisting backstage. The rest are helping in the front of house.

How many are helping in the front of house?

___6___   ✓

1 2 7
72   121
4 5   606
1̶2̶1̶
✗

7-8

The caterers at a concert make 728 meals.

Unfortunately 986 people turn up.

How many people go without a meal?

___162___   ✗

8 9 8 6
728
1̶6̶2̶

If an extra 300 meals are made, how many are left over?

___42___   ✓

9
10̶ 12 8
986
0 42

9

A bus starts at the terminus. It stops three times before it reaches the airport.

35 people get on at the terminus.

14 people get on at the school, 2 get off.

12 get on at the hospital and 16 get off.

6 get on in the High St and 28 get off.

How many people are on the bus when it arrives at the airport?   35   49   47

___21___   ✓

59   14 −   2 + 12
-16   49   47   59

+43   49
6   28
49   21

10

Sara buys some clothes worth £58.63.

As she spends over £50 she receives a £5 discount.

How much does she pay in total?

___£53.63___   ✓

Total

1

25	27	26	27	25	24	25
24	26	27	28	30	30	27

The midday temperatures in °C recorded over a fortnight are shown above.

What is the mode?

_____ 25 °C 27

2

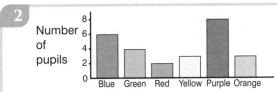

This graph shows the favourite colours of Year 5.

What is the modal colour?

_____ Purple ✓

3   Seven people's wages are listed below.

£110 £150 £120 £130 £140 £220 £435

What is the median wage?

Circle the answer.

A £143   B £435   C £186

D £140   E £130 ✓

4   The total attendance in one season for Cliffridge Football Club was 960 000.

They played 24 games.

What was the mean attendance? 24) 960 000

168,000   40   -199
                  -178
                   025

5

Month	May	June	July	Aug	Sep
Hours	174	186	191	199	188

Find the range for the hours of sunshine shown in the table above.

Circle the answer.

A 26   B 199   C 186   D 5   E 25 ✓

Time for a break! Go to Puzzle Page 42 ▶

6   6   4   2   0   8

Find the range of the numbers above.

Circle the answer.

A 8   B 0   C 4   D 6   E 20

7   8   6   2   1   13

Find the range of the numbers above.

Circle the answer.

A 13   B 1   C 12   D 8   E 30

8   12   7   20   5   19

What is the median of these numbers?

Circle the answer.

A 20   B 12   C 62   D 7   E 19 ✓

9

Day	Mon	Tues	Wed	Thurs	Fri
No. of cups	2		8	9	4

Heather thinks her mum is drinking too many cups of coffee a day.

Heather asks her some questions and completes this table.

Her mum says her mean is 7.

How many cups did she drink on Tuesday?

_____ 6   12.

10

Day	Mon	Tues	Wed	Thurs	Fri
Hours	12	13	8		4

Ali's dad thinks Ali is spending too many hours playing games on the computer.

His dad asks Ali some questions and completes this table.

Ali's dad says his mean is 9.

How many hours did Ali play games on Thursday?

_____ 8 ✓

Total [ ]

TEST 7: **Shape and Space**

1

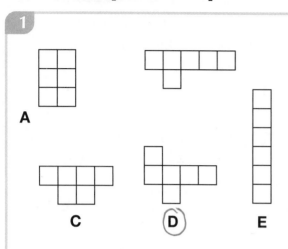

A

C   D   E

Look at the nets above.
Which one is the net of a closed cube?
Circle the answer.

2

All squares measure 30 cm by 30 cm.
What is the area of the entire pattern
in m²?
Circle the answer.

A 25.2 m²

B 2.52 m²

C 2520 m²

D 2.25 m²

E 22 500 m²

3

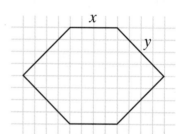

In the diagram above 1 square represents
1 cm².
What is the area of the parallelogram?
_____35_____ cm²

4

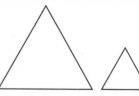

What is the correct formula for the area of
this shape?
Circle the answer.

A $2x^2$ **B** $(x + y)^2$

C $2x^2y^2$ **D** $\frac{1}{2}xy$

E $2x^2 + 2y^2$

5

The side length
of the smaller
equilateral triangle
is half the side
length of the larger equilateral triangle.
How many times will the smaller triangle fit
into the larger triangle?
Circle the answer.

2   3   (4)   5   6

6

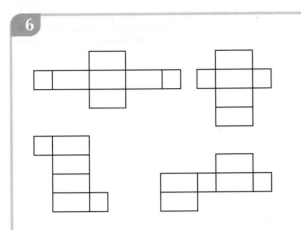

How many of the nets shown above will form a closed cuboid when folded?

Circle the answer.

A   None of them

B   Only 1 of them

C   2 of them

D   3 of them

E   All of them

7

What is the area of the triangle shown?

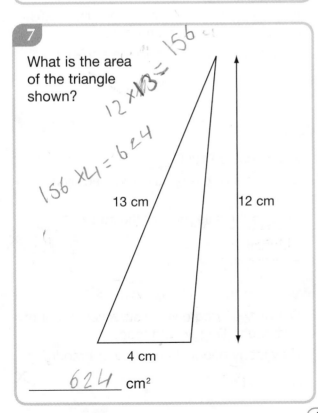

12 × 13 = 156

156 × 4 = 624

13 cm   12 cm

4 cm

_624_ cm²

8

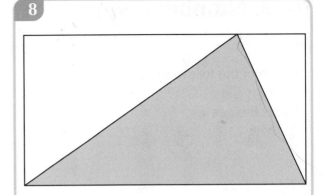

The area of the rectangle is 15 cm².
What is the area of the triangle?

_10_ cm²

9

The area of a rectangle is 70 cm.
What could be the perimeter of the rectangle?

Circle the answer.

A   7 cm

B   9 cm

C   12 cm

D   26 cm

E   34 cm

10

The perimeter of a rectangle is 24 cm.
If the rectangle is 10 cm long, what is the area of the rectangle?

Circle the answer.

A   10 cm²

B   11 cm²

C   20 cm²

D   32 cm²

E   220 cm²

Total

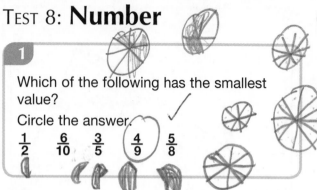

Test 8: Number

1

Which of the following has the smallest value?

Circle the answer. ✓

$\frac{1}{2}$ $\frac{6}{10}$ $\frac{3}{5}$ $\left(\frac{4}{9}\right)$ $\frac{5}{8}$

2

Which of the following has the largest value?

Circle the answer.

B   35 $\frac{3}{10}$

$\frac{2}{5}$ 20% $\frac{1}{3}$ $\left(35\%\right)$ 0.3   ✗

3

Which option is different from the others?

Circle the answer.

A $\frac{3}{4}$ of 200   150   **B** 75% of 200

C 0.75 of 200 150   **D** 0.5 of 400

E 150% of 100 ✗

4

Which option has the largest value?

Circle the answer.

A 62% of 60   **B** 0.63 of 60   **C** $\frac{3}{5}$ of 60

D $\frac{2}{3}$ of 60   **E** $\frac{5}{8}$ of 60 ✓

5

Jane scores 17 out of 25 in a maths test.

What percentage did she get?

75%   ✗   68%

6

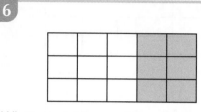

What percentage of the diagram is shaded?

40% ✓

7

Rowan has 50 marbles.

He gives 13 to Jack and keeps the rest.

What percentage does he keep for himself?

4   ✗

8

Ajay noticed that out of 400 buildings, 20% of them were terraced houses.

How many terraced houses are there?

80 ✓

9

1800   360

A sofa costs £1800.

During a sale the price is reduced by a third.

What is the sale price of the sofa?

3600   ✗

10

18 × 20 =

Out of 1400 dog owners surveyed, 8 out of 10 bought 'Doggy' dog food.

How many people bought other brands?

_____ ✗

Total

Test 9: **Shape and Space**

1-2

Below are 2 nets of open cuboids.
When each net is folded, it makes an open box.
What is the volume of each box?

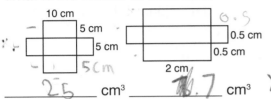

10 cm
5 cm
5 cm
5 cm

0.5 cm
0.5 cm
2 cm

_____25_____ cm³   _____1.7_____ cm³ ✗

3

6.20   6.30

What number does the arrow point to in the scale?

_____6.60_____ ✗

4

Tom buys three 2 litre bottles of water, 1.5 litres of milk and a 1 kg bag of potatoes.
What is the total weight of the shopping?
Circle the answer.

A 0.5 kg   **B** 2.5 kg   **C** 5.5 kg ✗

D 8.5 kg   **E** 10.5 kg

5

The weight limit for airline luggage is 25 kg.
A case weighs 25.80 kg.
An item weighing 850 g is removed.

25.80KG

How much does the case now weigh?
Circle the answer.

A 24.95 kg   **B** 26.65 kg   **C** 25.95 kg

D –825.80 kg **E** 17.30 kg   ✓

6

A tree is about 6 times the height of a tall man who is standing next to it.
Circle the answer that would be the closest to the height of the tree.

A 50 m   **B** 2000 mm   **C** 40 cm

D 5 mm   **E** 12 m

7

Tim buys a medium-sized rucksack.
Approximately how many litres will it hold?
Circle the answer.

A 0.5 litres   **B** 5 litres   **C** 50 litres

D 500 litres   **E** 5000 litres   ✗

8

Which container will hold about 30 litres?
Circle the correct letter.

A a bath   **B** a sink   **C** a kettle   ✗

D a milk bottle   **E** an egg cup

9

What is the area of this shape?

_____31_____ m²

5 m
2 m
8 m
10 m

10

The area of the shaded triangle is 1000 mm².
What is the area of the larger triangle?
Circle the answer.

A 90 000 mm² **B** 8000 mm² **C** 9.0 cm²

D 90 cm²   **E** 900 cm²

Total   1/10

Test time: 0   5   10 minutes

1

Out of 24 pairs of jeans, $\frac{2}{3}$ of them are blue.

3 ⌐

How many pairs of jeans are blue?

__16__   ✓

2

4

300 people are surveyed.

$\frac{2}{5}$ of them are 21 and under.   8.25

How many are 21 and under?

~~£8.75~~   120   ✗

3

25

~~250~~ people visit a coffee shop.

$\frac{3}{10}$ of the people order black coffee.   8 = 75

The rest order white coffee.   8 - 25° = 242

How many people order white coffee?

__242__   175   ✗

4

200 flights leave Abbeytown airport in one day.

5/200

$\frac{4}{5}$ are domestic and the rest are international.   160   40

How many flights are international?

40   160   40×4=   ✓

5

 14miles   2miles

In a 26-mile marathon, Gary sprints $\frac{1}{13}$ of the way, jogs $\frac{7}{13}$ of the way and walks the rest of the way.

How many miles does he walk for?

~~18~~ miles   10 miles ✗

6

The journey time from Greentown to Greenberg normally takes 40 minutes.

Due to traffic congestion, journey times have increased by 15%.

What is the new journey time?

__55__   46 ✓   ✗

7

Asima has £64.

She gives $\frac{1}{8}$ to Mary.   8

She gives $\frac{3}{8}$ to Jason.

The rest is given to Nabeel.

How much is Nabeel given?

£32   ✓

8

A shirt costs £30 before a '20% off everything' sale.

How much is the shirt in the sale?

__£25__   £24

9

2500

500 ml out of a 2.5 litre bottle of orange squash is concentrate.

What fraction is concentrate?

Circle the answer.

$\frac{1}{5}$ $\frac{1}{4}$ $\boxed{\frac{1}{3}}$ $\frac{1}{2}$ $\frac{1}{25}$ ✗

10 4000

4 kg of a certain type of food contains $\frac{1}{20}$

20 g of fat.   20/400 0

What fraction of the food is fat? $\frac{5}{100}$

__~~$\frac{5}{100}$~~__   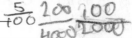   ✗

14

Total

TEST 11: Algebra

(handwritten: $6 = 24$ $\times 0 = 62$ $12 \times 2 = 42$)

1

I think of a number and multiply it by 4, then add 12. The answer I get is 76.
What number did I think of?

(handwritten: 18,2) *(handwritten: 64, 8, = 4√64)*

2

Gary has 21 marbles.
He has x red marbles.
He has three more blue marbles than red.
He has four times as many green as red.
How many red marbles does he have?

(handwritten: 8^7, $18 + 4 = 52$)

(handwritten: 4)

3

The numbers 1, 2, and 3 are consecutive.
Their sum is $1 + 2 + 3 = 6$.
The sum of another set of three consecutive whole numbers is 21.
Find the smallest of these numbers.

(handwritten: $18 \times 9 = 62 + 8 = $)

(handwritten: 6)

6

Akshay was x years old 5 years ago.
How old will he be in 7 years time?
Circle the answer.

A $x + 2$ **B** $x - 12$ **C** $12 - x$

(D) $12 + x$ **E** $x + 7$ *(D circled)*

7

y is $\frac{4}{5}$ of x.
Look at the list of statements below.
Circle the statement which is incorrect.

(A) $y = \frac{4}{5}x$ **B** $x = \frac{5}{4}y$ **C** $5y = 4x$ *(A circled)*

D $4y = 5x$ **E** $\frac{y}{x} = \frac{4}{5}$

8

A rectangle has a width x cm.
Its length is twice as long as its width.
Find an expression for the perimeter of the rectangle in terms of x.

(handwritten: 6x)

9

Minibuses have x seats. Coaches have y seats.
Bruce hires 2 minibuses and 7 coaches.
How many seats will there be in total?
Leave your answer in terms of x and y.

(handwritten: $7y + 2x$)

10

(handwritten: Do not understand)

If $7x - 9 = 10x - 18$, what is the value of x?

(handwritten: $\frac{23}{3}$) *(handwritten: $7x - 9 = 10x - 18$, $7x - 9$)*

Total

1

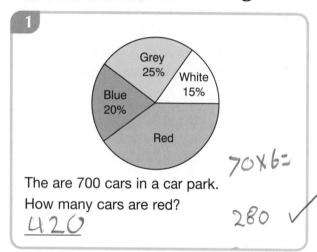

The are 700 cars in a car park.
How many cars are red?

__420__

70×6=

280 ✓

2

km

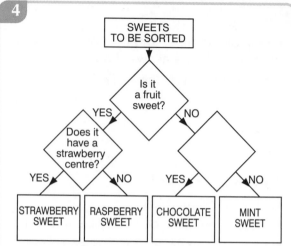

The graph shows the relationship between miles and kilometres.

Complete the following statement:

20 km is equivalent to __12.5__ miles. ✓

3

Alexander collected the following data from 100 pupils.

30
29
19
22

	Boys	Girls
Reggae	17	29
Hip Hop	13	7
Indipop	12	?

3o 19

How many girls prefer Indipop music?

__22__ ✓

4

SWEETS TO BE SORTED

Is it a fruit sweet?

YES   NO

Does it have a strawberry centre?

YES   NO   YES   NO

| STRAWBERRY SWEET | RASPBERRY SWEET | CHOCOLATE SWEET | MINT SWEET |

What is missing from the decision tree?
Circle the answer.

(A) Is it chocolate?   **B** Is it mint?

C IT IS MINT.   **D** IT IS CHOCOLATE.

E Is it not chocolate? ✓

5

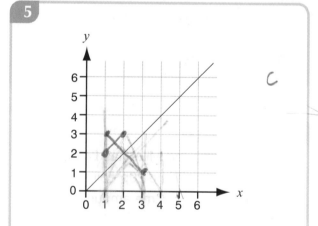

C

The end points of five lines are given below.
Which line is perpendicular to the line in the diagram?
Circle the answer.

A (1, 2) and (2, 2)   **B** (1, 3) and (3, 3)

C (3, 1) and (1, 3)   (D) (1, 4) and (4, 2)

E (5, 0) and (1, 3)

6

Bhavesh collected the following data from 100 pupils.

	Boys	Girls
English	19	7
Geography	4	?
Maths	38	30

How many girls preferred geography? 30

_____2_____ ✓

(margin working: 38, 11, 19)

7

A bag contains 8 red marbles, 2 green marbles and 10 black marbles.

You pick a marble at random from the bag.

In which of the options below are both statements true?

Circle the answer.

A You have a greater than even chance of picking a black marble.

You have a less than even chance of picking a green marble.

B You have an even chance of picking a black marble.

You have a greater than even chance of picking a red marble.

C You have a greater than even chance of picking a green marble.

You have an even chance of picking a black marble.

D You have a less than even chance of picking a red marble.

You have a less than even chance of picking a green marble.

E You are certain to pick a marble.

You have a greater than even chance of picking a black marble. ✓

8

Key: 🍫 = 10 bars   🍫 = 5 bars

Day	
Mon	🍫🍫 🍫🍫 🍫🍫 🍫
Tues	🍫🍫 🍫🍫 🍫
Wed	🍫🍫 🍫🍫 🍫🍫 🍫🍫
Thurs	🍫
Fri	🍫🍫 🍫🍫 🍫

Look at the pictogram above.
How many fruit bars were sold during the whole week?

_____135_____

(margin working: 35 ✓, 30, 40, 5, 25, 135)

9

Running 20%, Swimming 15%, Football 40%, Rowing

(margin working: 3.2, 6.4×7, 44.8 48, 75% to)

64 children were asked which sports they enjoyed.
How many children liked rowing? ✓

_____16_____

10

Look at this table showing the performance of the school cricket team.

Year	Won	Drawn	Lost	
2002	7	8	5	13
2003	13	2	5	7
2004	6	10	4	14

How many matches in total did the team not lose?

_____56_____

(margin working: 20, 36, 56, 44 ✗)

1 A coach holds 52 passengers.

12 fully-occupied coaches are required to transport fans to a football match.

How many fans travel by coach?

624 ✓

2 A crate can hold 24 cans.

Simon wants to order 312 cans.

How many crates should he order? ✓

13

3 A length of wood is 220 cm long.

It is cut into lengths of 30 cm.

How many complete pieces are made? ✓

7

4 2800 music fans attend a concert.

They travel in coaches. Each coach has 53 seats.

How many coaches are required?

560

(53) ✗

5

Pattern 1   Pattern 2   Pattern 3

How many tiles will be in Pattern 4?

16 ✓

6 Circle the multiple of both 5 and 7. ✓

A 12   **B** 57   **C** 14   **(D)** 35   **E** 15

7

Pattern 1   Pattern 2   Pattern 3

Pattern number	1	2	3	4
Grey tiles	1	2	3	4
White tiles	8	10	12	14
Total tiles	9	12	15	18

Which option correctly completes the details for Pattern 4?

Circle the answer.

A   Grey tiles = 4, White tiles = 12, total tiles = 16

B   Grey tiles = 3, White tiles = 14, total tiles = 17

C   Grey tiles = 4, White tiles = 12, total tiles = 17

(D) Grey tiles = 4, White tiles = 14, total tiles = 18

E   Grey tiles = 4, White tiles = 14, total tiles = 16   ✓

8 A drummer beats his drum once every four seconds.   4

A second drummer beats his drum once every five seconds.   5

They both start at the same time.

After how many more seconds do they beat their drums together again? ✗

5 beat. 20 seconds

9 What is the smallest number divisible by both 8 and 12?

48 24 ✓

10 What is the smallest number that is exactly divisible by 3 and 13?

39   12   26
       15   39 ✓

18

Total

Test time: 0 | | | | | 5 | | | | | 10 minutes

1

$4a + 2b - 7c = d.$

Find the value of d when $a = 5$, $b = 2$ and $c = 3$.

45

7 × 3 = 21
5 × 4 = 20
2 × 2 = 4

2

$4a + 2b + 3c = 20$

Which of the statements below is incorrect?

Circle the answer.

A $8a + 4b + 6c = 40$

B $4a + 2b = 20 - 3c$

C $4a + 2b + 3c - 20 = 0$

D $4a + 2b + 4c = 20 + c$

E $4a = 20 + 2b - 3c$

E

3

? → [ ] → 168

This machine doubles and then adds 2.

Which number has been put in?

83

33
50
83

4

The length of a rectangle is 8 cm more than its width. Its width is x cm.

A square has a side length of y cm.

The perimeter of the rectangle is larger than that of the square.

How much bigger is the perimeter of the rectangle than that of the square?

Circle the answer.

A $2x + 8 - y$ **B** $4x + 16 - 4y$

C $8x - 4y$ **D** $8xy$ **E** $2x + 8 - 4y$

5

If $17 - 16x = 3 - 2x$, what is the value of x?

+5

6

48 → [ ] → ?

This machine divides by 3 and then multiplies by 6.

Which number comes out?

96

16
6
36
66

3)48
16
18

7

If $3x + 2 = 2x + 7$, what is the value of x?

16   88

8

If $32 - x = 23 + 2x$, what is the value of x?

9

If Rose had 18 more stamps, she would have four times as many as she actually has.

How many stamps does she have?

88

10

A father's age and his son's age add up to 64. The father is 36 years older than his son.

How old is his son?

14

64
36
28

Total [ ]

TEST 15: **Shape and Space**

1–3

Guide the vehicles along the white squares from the start to the finish.

Each vehicle can only move FORWARD, TURN LEFT 90° and TURN RIGHT 90°.

1

Circle the correct instructions.

A FORWARD 3, TURN LEFT 90°,
FORWARD 2, TURN RIGHT 90°,
FORWARD 2, TURN LEFT 90°,
FORWARD 2, TURN RIGHT 90°,
FORWARD 3

B FORWARD 3, TURN RIGHT 90°,
FORWARD 2, TURN LEFT 90°,
FORWARD 2, TURN LEFT 90°,
FORWARD 2, TURN RIGHT 90°,
FORWARD 3

C FORWARD 3, TURN RIGHT 90°,
FORWARD 2, TURN RIGHT 90°,
FORWARD 2, TURN LEFT 90°,
FORWARD 2, TURN RIGHT 90°,
FORWARD 3

D FORWARD 3, TURN RIGHT 90°,
FORWARD 2, TURN RIGHT 90°,
FORWARD 2, TURN RIGHT 90°,
FORWARD 2, TURN RIGHT 90°,
FORWARD 3

E FORWARD 3, TURN LEFT 90°,
FORWARD 2, TURN LEFT 90°,
FORWARD 2, TURN LEFT 90°,
FORWARD 2, TURN LEFT 90°,
FORWARD 3

2

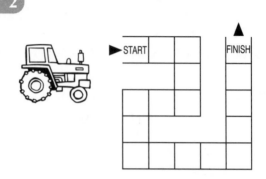

Circle the correct instructions.

A FORWARD 2, TURN RIGHT 90°,
FORWARD 2, TURN LEFT 90°,
FORWARD 2, TURN RIGHT 90°,
FORWARD 2, TURN LEFT 90°,
FORWARD 4, TURN LEFT 90°,
FORWARD 4

B FORWARD 2, TURN RIGHT 90°,
FORWARD 2, TURN RIGHT 90°,
FORWARD 2, TURN LEFT 90°,
FORWARD 2, TURN RIGHT 90°,
FORWARD 4, TURN LEFT 90°,
FORWARD 4

C FORWARD 2, TURN RIGHT 90°,
FORWARD 2, TURN RIGHT 90°,
FORWARD 2, TURN LEFT 90°,
FORWARD 2, TURN LEFT 90°,
FORWARD 4, TURN LEFT 90°,
FORWARD 4

D FORWARD 2, TURN RIGHT 90°,
FORWARD 2, TURN LEFT 90°,
FORWARD 2, TURN LEFT 90°,
FORWARD 2, TURN LEFT 90°,
FORWARD 4, TURN LEFT 90°,
FORWARD 4

E FORWARD 2, TURN LEFT 90°,
FORWARD 2, TURN RIGHT 90°,
FORWARD 2, TURN LEFT 90°,
FORWARD 2, TURN LEFT 90°,
FORWARD 4, TURN LEFT 90°,
FORWARD 4

3

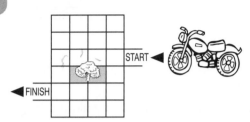

Circle the correct instructions.

A FORWARD 2, TURN LEFT 90°,
   FORWARD 3, TURN RIGHT 90°,
   FORWARD 1

B FORWARD 3, TURN LEFT 90°,
   FORWARD 2, TURN RIGHT 90°,
   FORWARD 2

C FORWARD 4, TURN LEFT 90°,
   FORWARD 2, TURN RIGHT 90°,
   FORWARD 1

D FORWARD 1, TURN LEFT 90°,
   FORWARD 4, TURN RIGHT 90°,
   FORWARD 1

E FORWARD 2, TURN LEFT 90°,
   FORWARD 2, TURN RIGHT 90°,
   FORWARD 3 ✓

4

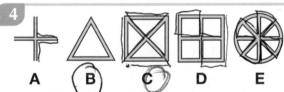

A papergirl does not want to visit the same street more than once.

She can pass over the same street corners.
On which housing estate is this possible?
Circle the answer. ✗

5

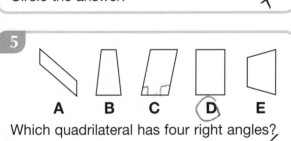

Which quadrilateral has four right angles?
Circle the answer. ✓

6

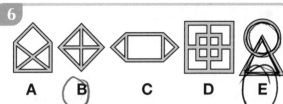

A postman does not want to visit the same street more than once.

He can pass over the same street corners.
On which housing estate is this possible?
Circle the answer. ✗

7

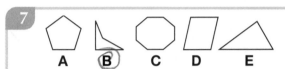

Which polygon has an internal reflex angle?
Circle the answer. ✓

8

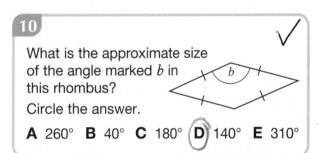

The diagram shows a rectangle joined to an equilateral triangle.
Find the size of the angle marked x.

____158____ ° ✓

9

One of the angles of this scalene triangle is 30°.
The other angle is 80°.
Find the size of the third angle marked a.

____70____ ° ✓

10 ✓

What is the approximate size of the angle marked b in this rhombus?
Circle the answer.

A 260° **B** 40° **C** 180° **D** 140° **E** 310°

Total

Test 16: **Mixed**

1

Given that $4x + 2y$ is the total cost in pounds for four adults and two children to enter a museum, which of the following statements is correct?

Circle the correct answer.

The cost for four adults and two children to enter the museum can also be written as:

A $8xy$ ✗   **B** $42xy$ ✗   **C** $6xy$ ✗

D $2(2x + y)$ **E** $8xy^2$

✗

2

Which letter shows two prime numbers that add up to make a square number?

Circle the answer.

A 12 and 13   **B** 17 and 19   **C** 16 and 20

D 16 and 8   **E** 1 and 35

✓

3

18

435 pupils are put into classes of 23 pupils.

How many complete classes are there?

_____ 11

$23\overline{)435}$

25

4

$6x + 7 = 28$

If $6x + 7 = 28 - x$, what is the value of x?

_____ 6

82
60 ✗
60
60
60

5

How many minutes are there in total in 4 hours and 32 minutes?

_____ 272

✓

6

Kevin wants to estimate the length of a room.

It takes him 15 strides to walk the length of the room.

What is the approximate length of the room?

Circle the answer.

A 40 m   **B** 1400 mm   **C** 1400 cm

D 200 cm   **E** 3 km

✗

7

The cost of a ham roll is £x and the cost of a tuna salad is £y.

Brian orders 5 ham rolls and 3 tuna salads.

What is a correct expression for the total cost of his order?

Circle the answer.

A $53xy$ **B** $5x + 3y$ **C** $15xy$

D $8xy$ **E** $15(x + y)$

✗

8

Write in words the number 14 205.

fourteen thousand two hundred and five ✓

9

4.3201

What is this number to two decimal places?

_4.32_

21
7
22 ✓

10

14

14 9 22 7 21

These are the number of letters received by a library each day for a week.

What is the median number of letters?

_14_ ~~7~~ ✓

Total

[handwritten: 11.02 ×6 / 5, 27]

1

Here is part of a conversion table.
Which figure is missing from the table?

lbs	g	kg	lbs
5	2270	5	11.02
6	2720	6	?
7	3180	7	15.43
8	3630	8	17.64

[handwritten: 2.204, 11.02, 13.23]

[handwritten under table: 2.72, 2.72]

[handwritten: 13.23 ✗]

2

13 14 (15) 16 18

Circle the number which is divisible by both 3 and 5. ✓

3

[handwritten: 180]

What proportion of 3 hours is 10 minutes?
Circle the answer. *[handwritten: 1/18]*

A $\frac{1}{3}$ B $\frac{1}{6}$ (C) $\frac{1}{18}$ D $\frac{1}{9}$ (E) $\frac{1}{12}$ ✗

4

DUD   FUF   (EEE)   POP   DOL

Which of these has a horizontal line of symmetry? Circle the answer. ✓

5–6

Where is the court?

(_2_, _12_) ✓

Where is the fire station?

(_8_, _3_) ✓

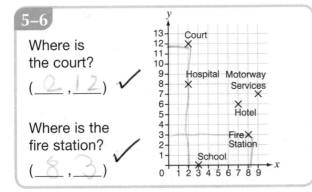

7

64 → [÷8] → [×5] → _____

[handwritten: 40 ✓]

Complete the function machine.

8

Edward has these coins in his pocket.

1p 2p 5p 10p 10p 10p 10p £1

He selects a coin at random.

In which of the options below are both statements true?

Circle the answer.

A He has an even chance of picking a 10p coin out.
He has an even chance of picking a coin less than 10p out.

(B) He has a less than even chance of picking a 2p coin out.
He has a less than even chance of picking a 5p coin out. ✓

C He has an even chance of picking a 1p coin out.
He is certain to pick a coin of value £1 or less.

D He has an even chance of picking a 10p coin out.
He has an even chance of picking a coin out greater than 10p.

E He is certain to pick a coin out that is less than £1.
He has a less than even chance of picking a coin out that is less than 10p.

9

Which of these will hold about 10 litres?

Circle the answer.

A a teaspoon   **B** a cup

C a swimming pool   **(D)** a bucket   ✓

E a lake

10

What fraction is 10 mm of 30 cm? ✗

Circle the answer.

A $\frac{1}{3}$ **B** $\frac{1}{30}$ **C** $\frac{10}{30}$ **(D)** $\frac{1}{300}$ **E** $\frac{1}{0.3}$

[handwritten: B]

[handwritten: 10mm = 1cm = 1/30]

Total [_____]

1

A length of wire is d cm long.

It is cut to form an equilateral triangle of side x cm **and** a square of side y cm.

The perimeter of the equilateral triangle and the square are the same.

Read these statements.

> Statement 1: $6x = d$
>
> Statement 2: $8y = d$
>
> Statement 3: $4x + 3y = d$

Circle the answer.

A All of the statements are correct.

B Only statement 3 is correct.

C Only statements 1 and 2 are correct. ✓

2

Sam buys some apples which cost 27p each.

He pays for them with three one pound coins.

Kay buys the same number of bananas which cost 37p each.

She pays for them with four one pound coins.

They each receive the same amount of change.

How many pieces of fruit did each person buy?

16 £3.70 £2.70 ✓

3

A canteen makes 456 pies.

They sell 322.

How many pies remain?

456

134 ✓

4

Guide the robot through the kitchen without hitting any hazards.

He can only move FORWARD, TURN LEFT 90° and TURN RIGHT 90°.

Circle the correct instructions.

A FORWARD 1, TURN RIGHT 90°,
FORWARD 1, TURN RIGHT 90°,
FORWARD 1

B FORWARD 2, TURN LEFT 90°,
FORWARD 1, TURN RIGHT 90°,
FORWARD 3

C FORWARD 2, TURN RIGHT 90°,
FORWARD 1, TURN LEFT 90°,
FORWARD 2, TURN LEFT 90°,
FORWARD 2, TURN RIGHT 90°,
FORWARD 1

D FORWARD 3, TURN RIGHT 90°,
FORWARD 1, TURN LEFT 90°,
FORWARD 2, TURN LEFT 90°,
FORWARD 1, TURN RIGHT 90°,
FORWARD 1

E FORWARD 3, TURN LEFT 90°,
FORWARD 1, TURN LEFT 90°,
FORWARD 2, TURN LEFT 90°,
FORWARD 2, TURN RIGHT 90°,
FORWARD 1

5

Here is part of a conversion table. Which figure is missing from the table?

ft	m		m	ft
5	1.53		5	16.40
6	1.83		6	?
7	2.13		7	22.97
8	2.44		8	26.25

Circle the answer.

A 18.23 ft

B 19.01 ft

C 19.68 ft

D 15.33 ft

E 16.40 ft

6

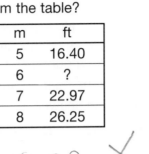

Of 55 households surveyed, how many used most of their water for washing?

7

What is the perimeter of the room?

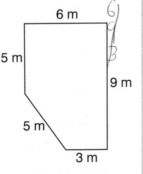

_____ m

6 m

5 m

9 m

5 m

3 m

8

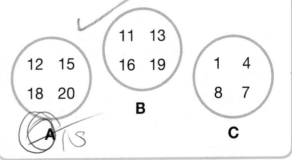

Look at the graph to show the temperature conversion between Fahrenheit (°F) and Celsius (°C).

Use your graph to work out how many degrees Fahrenheit are equivalent to 30°.

Circle the answer.

A 0   **B** 90   **C** 80   **D** 86   **E** 76

9

Iris withdraws £1300 from her bank account.

She is given the money in £20 notes.

How many £20 notes does she have in total?

10

Which circle contains only multiples of either 3 or 5?

Circle the answer.

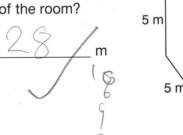

12   15
18   20

A

11   13
16   19

B

1   4
8   7

C

Total

1

The probability that Mr Yang will catch the bus to school is 0.4.

The probability he will walk is 0.2.

Otherwise he will drive to school.

0.4

What is the chance that he will drive to school?

_____0.4_____ ✓

2

A piece of wood 6 m 18 cm long is to be cut into three equal pieces.

How long will each piece be?   2

Circle the answer.

A 3 m 6 cm   **B** 2 m 60 cm   **C** 3 m 0.6 cm

D 306 m   (**E**) 206 cm ✓

3

zon   sno oson   on2   SOA

NOZ   ONS   NSO   ZNO   (NOS)

Which of these makes a word when rotated through 180°?

Circle the correct word. ✓

4

$\frac{3}{12} = \frac{1}{4}$

What fraction of 3 hours is 45 minutes?

$\frac{9}{12}$ $\frac{9}{12} = \frac{3}{4}$ $3 \times 3 = 9$ $4 \times 3 = 12$

5

174
47 6

Jen wants to save two files onto CD.

One file is 68 MB. The other is 96 MB.   68

A CD can hold 650 MB.   68 a b
                          1 74

How many MB of space will be left on the CD once she has saved both files?

_____476 MB_____ ✗

486 MB

6

Reflecting this scalene triangle in its dashed side, will make a quadrilateral.

What is the name of this quadrilateral?

Circle the answer.

A Square   **B** Rectangle   **C** Rhombus

(**D**) Parallelogram ✗   (**E**) Kite ✓

7

If $4x - 2 = 2x + 8$, what is the value of x?

_____8_____ $2x - 2 = 8$ ✗ ✓

8

1.5
0.8

Daxa buys two 1.5 litre cartons of juice, 3 litres of milk and a 500 g jar of coffee.

Approximately what is the total weight of the shopping?

Circle the answer.

A 0.5 kg   **B** 1.5 kg   **C** 2.5 kg

D 5.5 kg   (**E**) 6.5 kg ✗

$\frac{12}{21}$
70
100
30

9

Amanda plants 17 rows and 13 columns of cabbage plants in a rectangular pattern.

How many cabbage plants has she planted altogether?

_____22 (_____

17
13
___
5 1
1 7 0
___
1

✓

10

? → [ ] → 94   94

This machine triples and then adds 7.

Which number has been put in?

_____29_____   29   3)87   27

(26)

Total   6.

TEST 20:

1

$\frac{1}{4}$ $\frac{3}{8}$ $\frac{2}{5}$ $\frac{2}{7}$ $\frac{7}{32}$

Which of these fractions has the lowest value?

Circle the answer.

2

Given that $3x + 9y = 6z$,

what is the value of $x + 3y = $?

Give the answer in terms of z.

_____

3

When the net is folded to make the cuboid, which corner will join to corner L?

_____

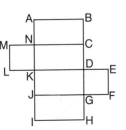

4

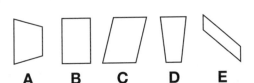

A   B   C   D   E

Which quadrilateral does not have an obtuse angle?

Circle the answer.

5

In Grange School, girls and boys are in the ratio 8 : 9.

There are 72 boys, how many girls are there?

_____

6

Norbert is 2 metres 0 centimetres tall.

Which is the closest to his height in feet and inches?

Circle the answer.

A 5 feet 11 inches   **B** 6 feet 1 inch

C 6 feet 3 inches   **D** 6 feet 5 inches

E 6 feet 7 inches

7

Find the coordinates of points P, Q and R.

P (___, ___)

Q (___, ___)

R (___, ___)

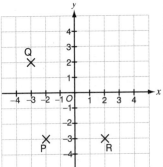

8

£420 is raised at a Funday.

$\frac{6}{7}$ of the money is donated to charity.

The rest is kept as profit.

How much profit is made?

_____

9 $4x - 2y = z$.

Find the value of x when $y = 7$ and $z = 2$.

_____

10   121 → ÷11 → ×12 → _____

Complete the function machine.

Total [   ]

1

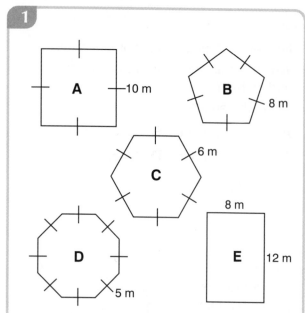

Which shape has a different perimeter from the others?

_____

2

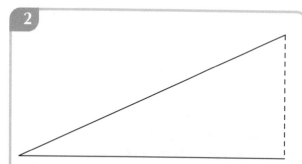

Reflecting this right-angled triangle in its dashed side will make another triangle.

What is the name of this triangle?

Circle the answer.

A Equilateral

B Scalene

C Isosceles

D Right-angled

E Regular

3

Lauren was carrying a 620 g bag of potatoes, and two 200 g bags of fruit.

The total weight of Peter's bags was exactly half the total weight of Lauren's bags.

How much weight did Peter carry?

_____ g

4

Miss Drake is 6 feet 0 inches tall.

Which is the closest to her height in metres?

Circle the answer.

A 1.7 m   **B** 1.8 m   **C** 1.9 m

D 2.0 m   **E** 2.1 m

5

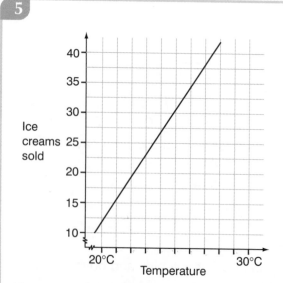

How many ice creams were sold when the temperature was 26°C?

_____

6

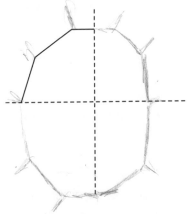

The diagram shows part of a shape and two lines of symmetry.

What is the name of the complete shape?

Circle the answer.

A Regular hexagon 6

B Regular octagon 8

C Regular dodecagon 12

D Regular decagon 10

E Irregular dodecagon 12

7

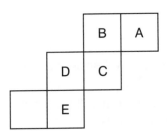

Look at this net of a closed cube.

Which side will be directly opposite the unmarked side, when it is folded to make the cube?

Circle the answer.

A   **B**   **C**   **D**   **E**

8

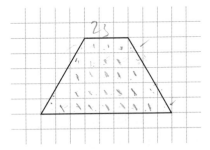

In the diagram above 1 square represents 1 cm².

What is the area of the trapezium?

_____ cm²

9

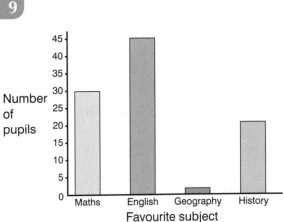

How many people like the most popular subject?

_____

10

May pays a £700 deposit towards a car costing £3899.

She saves £457 per month toward the total cost.

How many months does it take her to save the rest of the money?

_____

Total [   ]

Test time: 0 | | | | | 5 | | | | | 10 minutes

1

In which number is the 7 worth seven hundred?

Circle the answer.

A 70 608   **B** 83 768   **C** 1127

D 103 872   **E** 47 316

2

What fraction of 1 hour is 40 minutes?

Leave your answer in its simplest form.

_____

3

$5 \times 5 \times 5 \times 5 \times 5 \times 5 = ?$

Circle the answer.

A 5^6 **B** 30   **C** 6^5 **D** 555 555   **E** 56

4

The sides labelled x are the same length.

How many times will the small right-angled triangle fit into the octagon?

_____

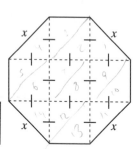

5

Ian sends 12 text messages daily costing 4p each.

He makes 4 calls each day costing 20p each.

How much does he spend altogether over five days?

_____

6

Which of these has a horizontal line of symmetry?

Circle the answer.

HIM   MIM   TIM   LIN   HIH

7

Cindy has to pay £1 to enter a fair.

She only has one type of coin.

Circle the option which she could not use.

A One £1 coin   **B** Two 50p coins

C Four 25p coins   **D** Five 20p coins

E Ten 10p coins

8

The area of a square is 64 cm².

What is the perimeter of the square?

Circle the answer.

A 16 cm   **B** 9 cm   **C** 32 cm

D 50 cm   **E** 64 cm

9

The probability it will snow on Christmas Day 2020 is 0.02.

What is the chance it will not snow on Christmas Day 2020?

_____

10

What is the area of the shape?

_____ m²

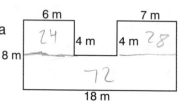

Total

TEST 23: **Mixed**

Test time: 0 .... 5 .... 10 minutes

1

What is the six in the number 7608 worth?

_____

2

Una sells ice lollies for 45p and ice cream cones for 32p.
She sells 34 of the ice lollies and 12 cones.
How much does she make altogether?

£_____

3 The perimeter of a rectangle is 50 cm.
If the rectangle is 20 cm long, what is the area of the rectangle?
Circle the answer.

A 40 cm²　**B** 70 cm²　**C** 60 cm²

D 250 cm²　**E** 100 cm²

4

Which ratio is not the same as the ratio 14 : 20?
Circle the answer.

A 7 : 10　**B** 2 : $\frac{20}{7}$　**C** 1 : $\frac{10}{7}$

D 28 : 40　**E** 10 : 16

5

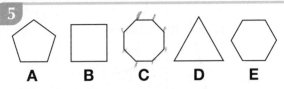

A　B　C　D　E

An angle inside a polygon is called an interior angle.
Which one of the above regular polygons has an interior angle of 135°?
Circle the answer.

6

A train leaves London at 13.47. The journey to Leeds takes 2 hours and 29 minutes. What time does it arrive in Leeds?

_____

7

Which number is divisible by 12 and 24?
Circle the answer.

A 12　**B** 36　**C** 48　**D** 60　**E** 80

8

Find the size of the unmarked angle.

_____ °

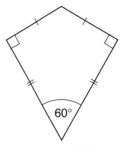

60°

9

Jennie collected money for a charity.
One morning she received the following donations:
£1.64　£2.12　£0.89　20p　£3.45
She collected £34 in the afternoon.
How much did she collect in total?

_____

10

Which of the following fractions has the smallest value?
Circle the answer.

$\frac{2}{3}$　　$\frac{4}{10}$　　$\frac{5}{8}$　　$\frac{1}{6}$　　$\frac{7}{10}$

Total

1

Which of the following has the largest value?

Circle the answer.

$\frac{5}{7}$ 71%   0.69 $\frac{2}{3}$ 65%

2

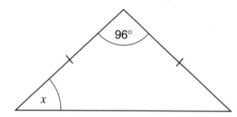

37.1   37.2

What number does the arrow point to?

_____

3

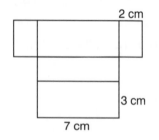

96°

x

Find the size of the angle marked x in this isosceles triangle.

_____ °

4

2 cm

3 cm

7 cm

This is a net of an open cuboid.
It is then folded to make an open box.
What is the volume of the box?

_____ cm³

5

Mike is using a map where 1 cm represents 2 km.
His walk is 8 cm on the map.
How far will his actual walk be?

_____ km

6

Name	Bank Balance
Mr Spend	−£145
Mr Save	−£468
Mr Broke	£12
Mr Rich	£567
Mr Debt	−£222
Miss Out	£879

The table above shows the balance of six people's bank accounts.
Who owes the most money?

_____

7

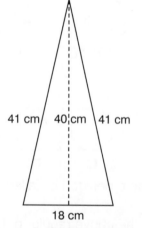

41 cm   40 cm   41 cm

18 cm

What is the area of the triangle?

_____ cm²

Guide the car along the white squares on the plan from the start to the finish.

It can only move FORWARD, TURN RIGHT 90° and TURN LEFT 90°.

Circle the correct instructions.

A FORWARD 3, TURN LEFT 90°,
FORWARD 3, TURN LEFT 90°,
FORWARD 2, TURN LEFT 90°,
FORWARD 4, TURN RIGHT 90°,
FORWARD 2, TURN RIGHT 90°,
FORWARD 2, TURN LEFT 90°,
FORWARD 1

B FORWARD 3, TURN RIGHT 90°,
FORWARD 2, TURN LEFT 90°,
FORWARD 2, TURN LEFT 90°,
FORWARD 4, TURN RIGHT 90°,
FORWARD 2, TURN RIGHT 90°,
FORWARD 2, TURN LEFT 90°,
FORWARD 1

C FORWARD 3, TURN LEFT 90°,
FORWARD 3, TURN LEFT 90°,
FORWARD 2, TURN LEFT 90°,
FORWARD 4, TURN LEFT 90°,
FORWARD 2, TURN RIGHT 90°,
FORWARD 3, TURN LEFT 90°,
FORWARD 1

D FORWARD 3, TURN RIGHT 90°,
FORWARD 2, TURN LEFT 90°,
FORWARD 2, TURN LEFT 90°,
FORWARD 4, TURN RIGHT 90°,
FORWARD 2, TURN RIGHT 90°,
FORWARD 3, TURN RIGHT 90°,
FORWARD 1

E FORWARD 3, TURN RIGHT 90°,
FORWARD 2, TURN LEFT 90°,
FORWARD 2, TURN LEFT 90°,
FORWARD 4, TURN RIGHT 90°,
FORWARD 2, TURN LEFT 90°,
FORWARD 2, TURN RIGHT 90°,
FORWARD 1

9

Which of the statements is correct?
Circle the answer.

A *b* and *c* are parallel

B *a* and *b* are vertical

C *e* is vertical

D *d* is horizontal

E *a* and *b* are parallel

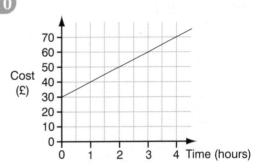

How much does Ben charge for a plumbing job lasting 4 hours?

_____

Total

TEST 25: **Mixed**

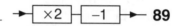

1

Which number completes the list in order of size?

0.038, ...,   0.042

Circle the answer.

0.0379   0.4   0.04   0.004   0.39

2

A submarine descends from sea level (0 m) to a depth of 150 m.

It then rises 76 m.

How far is it below sea level now?

_____ m below sea level.

3

Which of these makes a word when rotated through 180°?

Circle the answer.

NOOS   ENO   ONNS   ENNA   OOB

4

Which answer is different from the others?

Circle the answer.

A 0.1 of 20   **B** 10% of 20   **C** $\frac{1}{10}$ of 20

D 20% of 10   **E** 0.01 of 20

5

How many Fentos are equivalent to 25 Pentos?

_____ Fentos

6

Complete the function machine.

_____ → [×2] [−1] → **89**

7

This is a net of an open cube.
It is folded to make an open box.
What is the volume of the box?

_____ cm³

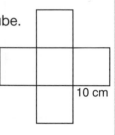

10 cm

8

Which two of these polygons have diagonals that cross at right angles?

Circle the answers.

A Trapezium   **B** Square

C Rhombus   **D** Regular pentagon

E Rectangle

9

Which is the first number greater than 100 that is divisible by both 3 and 6?

_____

10

Jake is driving at a speed of 64 kmh or 40 mph.

Lee is cycling at a speed of 32 kmh or 20 mph.

Roger is travelling on a motorbike at a speed of 96 kmh.

What is his speed in mph?

_____ mph

Total

1

```
+--+--+--+--+--+--+--+--+--+--+--+--+--+
0           2        ↑        4
```

What number does the arrow point to?

_____

2

Complete the function machine.

72 → ÷6 → ×15 → _____

3

Which of the following will hold about 5 ml?
Circle the answer.

A a teaspoon   **B** a swimming pool

C a mug   **D** a bucket

E a reservoir

4

The area of a rectangle is 30 cm².
Which could be the perimeter of the
rectangle?
Circle the answer.

A 6 cm   **B** 9 cm   **C** 12 cm

D 22 cm   **E** 28 cm

5

What is the difference between 9°C and
−2°C?

_____ °C

6 5.9945

Write this number to two decimal places.

_____

7

A school sells 700 concert tickets for £3.99
each.
How much money did they raise?

_____

8

Sue thinks of a positive number, multiplies
it by itself and then halves the answer.
The number she ends up with is 18.
What was her original number?

_____

9

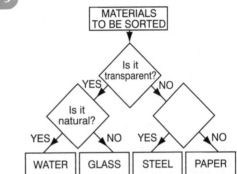

What is missing from the decision tree?
Circle the answer.

A IT IS WEAK.   **B** IT IS STRONG.

C IT IS TRANSPARENT.   **D** Is it strong?

E Is it opaque?

10

In a maths test Andy gets 30 out of the 35
questions correct.
What proportion has he got right?
Circle the answer.

$\frac{5}{7}$ $\frac{6}{7}$ $\frac{3}{5}$ $\frac{3}{4}$ $\frac{5}{6}$

Total

1

A map has a scale of 1 : 25 000.

What does 4 cm on the map represent in actual distance?

Circle the answer.

A 25 m

B 25 km

C 100 m

D 100 km

E 1 km

2

| 1 | 2 | 3 | 4 | 5 |

Which of the statements is incorrect?

Circle the answer.

A 2, 3 and 5 are parallel

B 2, 3 and 5 are vertical

C 1 and 4 are parallel

D 1 is perpendicular to 2

E 5 is horizontal

3

The time in Thornsburg is 6 hours ahead of London.

The time in London is 8.27 pm.

What is the time in Thornsburg?

Circle the answer.

A 2.27 pm   **B** 14.27

C 02.27 pm   **D** 02.27

E 14.27 am

4

Guide the robot through the grid without hitting any animals.

He can only move FORWARD, TURN LEFT 90° and TURN RIGHT 90°.

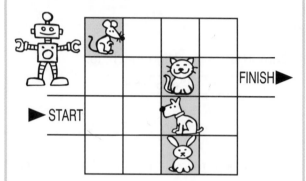

Circle the correct instructions.

A FORWARD 4, TURN LEFT 90°, FORWARD 1, TURN RIGHT 90°, FORWARD 1

B FORWARD 1, TURN LEFT 90°, FORWARD 2, TURN RIGHT 90°, FORWARD 2, TURN RIGHT 90°, FORWARD 1, TURN LEFT 90°, FORWARD 2

C FORWARD 1, TURN LEFT 90°, FORWARD 2, TURN RIGHT 90°, FORWARD 2, TURN RIGHT 90°, FORWARD 2, TURN LEFT 90°, FORWARD 1

D FORWARD 2, TURN LEFT 90°, FORWARD 2, TURN RIGHT 90°, FORWARD 2, TURN RIGHT 90°, FORWARD 1, TURN LEFT 90°, FORWARD 1

E FORWARD 2, TURN LEFT 90°, FORWARD 2, TURN RIGHT 90°, FORWARD 2, TURN RIGHT 90°, FORWARD 2, TURN LEFT 90°, FORWARD 1

5

An ammeter shows current of 4 amps (A).

There are 1000 mA to 1 amp.

The current drops by 500 mA.

What reading does the ammeter now show?

_____ A

6

Convert the list below to fractions and find the smallest fraction.

Circle the answer.

A 30 minutes as a fraction of 2 hours

B 20 minutes as a fraction of 3 hours

C 15 minutes as a fraction of 2 hours

D 40 minutes as a fraction of 1 hour

E 10 minutes as a fraction of 1 hour

7

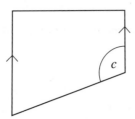

What is the approximate size of the angle marked *c* in the trapezium?

Circle the answer.

A 150°

B 110°

C 90°

D 60°

E 300°

8

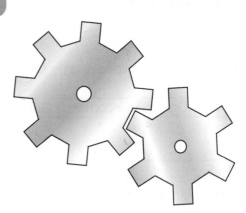

The cog with 8 grooves makes 12 complete revolutions.

How many complete revolutions will the cog with 6 grooves have made?

_____

9

Complete the function machine.

27 → [×7] [÷3] →

_____

10

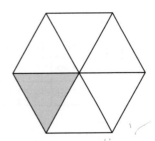

How many more triangles need to be shaded so 50% of the hexagon is shaded?

Circle the answer.

1   2   3   4   5

Total [   ]

Test time: 0 | | | | | 5 | | | | 10 minutes

1

John collected the following data from 100 children.

	Drum	Recorder	Guitar
Boys	3	?	12
Girls	23	18	18

How many boys gave the recorder as their favourite instrument?

_____

2

Lia thinks of a positive number.

She multiplies it by itself and gets 144.

What was the number she started with?

_____

3

14 000 people each pay £25 for a concert ticket.

How much money is raised?

£_____

4

What is the missing number?

135	148	109
122	?	148
109	122	135

_____

5

Out of 600 people interviewed, 378 liked watching soap operas.

What percentage of people surveyed liked watching soap operas?

_____

6

Pat collected the following data from 100 pupils.

	Tennis	Judo	Ballet
Boys	13	1	18
Girls	54	3	?

How many girls gave ballet as their favourite activity?

_____

7

This is a net of an open cuboid. It is then folded to make an open box.

What is the volume of the box?

_____ cm³

0.3 cm

0.6 cm

0.2 cm

8

A   B   C   D   E

Which shape has 3 edges less than shape D?

_____

9

Lara usually buys 150 g bags of crisps.

She sees a bag which is 30% larger.

What is the weight of the large bag?

_____ g

10

If p is $\frac{3}{4}$ of q, what is $3q$?

_____

38

Total

Answers

TEST 1: Shape and Space

1 $\frac{1}{8}$
2 C
3 B
4 (8.2, 8.5)
5 (6, 7)
6 (5, 8)
7 A
8 C
9 E
10 (2, –2)

TEST 4: Data Handling

1 40
2 A
3 5
4 28
5 7
6 23
7 C
8 B
9 $\frac{21}{23}$
10 0.75 or $\frac{3}{4}$ or 75%

TEST 7: Shape and Space

1 D
2 D
3 35
4 A
5 4
6 D
7 24
8 7.5
9 E
10 C

TEST 2: Number

1 A
2 90 909
3 E
4 A
5 300 or 3 hundreds
6 7.006
7 $\frac{2}{3}$
8 $\frac{4}{5}$
9 7.63
10 9.00

TEST 5: Number

1 15
2 1
3 A
4 4
5 283
6 6
7 258
8 42
9 21
10 £53.63

TEST 8: Number

1 $\frac{4}{9}$
2 $\frac{2}{5}$
3 D
4 D
5 68%
6 40%
7 74%
8 80
9 £1200
10 280

TEST 3: Shape and Space

1 D
2 E
3 SIH
4 D
5 LAL
6 DID
7 44
8 32
9 D
10 A

TEST 6: Data Handling

1 27
2 Purple
3 D
4 40 000
5 E
6 A
7 C
8 B
9 12
10 8

TEST 9: Shape and Space

1 250
2 0.5
3 6.26
4 D
5 A
6 E
7 C
8 B
9 70
10 D

Test 10: **Number**

1 16
2 120
3 175
4 40
5 10
6 46 minutes
7 £32
8 £24
9 $\frac{1}{5}$
10 $\frac{1}{200}$

Test 11: **Algebra**

1 16
2 3
3 6
4 3
5 17
6 D
7 D
8 $6x$
9 $2x + 7y$
10 3

Test 12: **Data Handling**

1 280
2 12.5 accept 12 or 13
3 22
4 A
5 C
6 2
7 D
8 135
9 16
10 46

Test 13: **Number**

1 624
2 13
3 7
4 53
5 16
6 D
7 D
8 20
9 24
10 39

Test 14: **Algebra**

1 3
2 E
3 83
4 B
5 1
6 96
7 5
8 3
9 6
10 14

Test 15: **Shape and Space**

1 B
2 C
3 C
4 B
5 D
6 E
7 B
8 150
9 70
10 D

Test 16: **Mixed**

1 D
2 B
3 18
4 3
5 272
6 C
7 B
8 Fourteen thousand, two hundred and five
9 4.32
10 14

Test 17: **Mixed**

1 13.23
2 15
3 C
4 EEE
5 (2, 12)
6 (8, 3)
7 40
8 B
9 D
10 B

Test 18: **Mixed**

1 C
2 10
3 134
4 C
5 C
6 22
7 28
8 D
9 65
10 A

Test 19: **Mixed**

1 0.4
2 E
3 NOS
4 $\frac{1}{4}$
5 486
6 E
7 5
8 E
9 221
10 29

Test 22: **Mixed**

1 B
2 $\frac{2}{3}$
3 A
4 14
5 £6.40
6 HIH
7 C
8 C
9 0.98
10 124

Test 25: **Mixed**

1 0.04
2 74
3 NOOS
4 E
5 5
6 45
7 1000
8 B and C
9 102
10 60

Test 20: **Mixed**

1 $\frac{7}{32}$
2 $2z$
3 J
4 B
5 64
6 E
7 P(–2, –3) Q(–3, 2) R(2, –3)
8 £60
9 4
10 132

Test 23: **Mixed**

1 600
2 £19.14
3 E
4 E
5 C
6 16:16
7 C
8 120
9 £42.30
10 $\frac{1}{6}$

Test 26: **Mixed**

1 3.2
2 180
3 A
4 D
5 11
6 5.99
7 £2793
8 6
9 D
10 $\frac{6}{7}$

Test 21: **Mixed**

1 C
2 C
3 510
4 B
5 34
6 D
7 C
8 30
9 45
10 7

Test 24: **Mixed**

1 $\frac{5}{7}$
2 37.18
3 42
4 42
5 16
6 Mr Save
7 360
8 B
9 E
10 £70

Test 27:

1 E
2 E
3 D
4 D
5 3.5
6 B
7 B
8 16
9 63
10 2

TEST 28: Mixed

1 26
2 12
3 £350 000
4 135
5 63%
6 11
7 0.036
8 C
9 195
10 $4p$

TEST 29: Mixed

1 50 000
2 B
3 $\frac{4}{5}$
4 B
5 $50x + 20y$
6 6.63
7 16
8 D
9 15
10 116 or 117

TEST 30: Mixed

1 $y + 15$
2 Thursday
3 144
4 A
5 210
6 45
7 38
8 15
9 $\frac{1}{2}$ or 0.5 or 50%
10 E

Puzzle ❶

204

a 8 different sizes
b $8 \times 8 = 64$ of the 1 by 1 squares
c $1 \times 1 = 1$ of the 8 by 8 squares
   $2 \times 2 = 4$ of the 7 by 7 squares
   $3 \times 3 = 9$ of the 6 by 6 squares
   $4 \times 4 = 16$ of the 5 by 5 squares
   $5 \times 5 = 25$ of the 4 by 4 squares
   $6 \times 6 = 36$ of the 3 by 3 squares
   $7 \times 7 = 49$ of the 2 by 2 squares
   $64 + 49 + 36 + 25 + 16 + 9 + 4 + 1 = 204$

Puzzle ❷

a 1, 4, 9, 16, 25
b Square numbers

Puzzle ❸

	1	2			5	5
5		3	6		2	7
6	5		6	1		7
	8	7		9	1	
4		4	3		4	9
2	9		8	3		2
	6	7		4	8	

Puzzle ❹

cat	mouse	owl	cat	30
owl	mouse	cat	mouse	27
owl	mouse	cat	owl	31
cat	mouse	mouse	cat	26
34	20	30	30	

Puzzle ❺

1 kg, 2 kg, 4 kg, 8 kg, 16 kg

1

The table below shows the atmospheric temperature at different altitudes.

Altitude above sea level (ft)	Temperature (°C)
1 000	10
2 000	8
5 000	2
15 000	−8
20 000	−23
50 000	−67

Which altitude is the coldest?

_____ ft

2

What is the size of the angle marked b in the isosceles triangle?

Circle the answer.

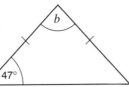

A 266° **B** 86° **C** 96° **D** 47° **E** 153°

3

Mia travels 40 miles before she has a rest.

Her total journey is 50 miles.

What fraction of her journey has she completed?

_____

4

Find the range for the hours of sunshine shown in the table.

Month	May	June	July	Aug	Sep
Hours	172	171	189	197	186

Circle the answer.

A 171 **B** 26 **C** 184 **D** 5 **E** 25

5

Kim is ordering some stationery.

She orders x boxes of pencils each containing 50 pencils.

She orders y boxes of pens each containing 20 pens.

How many items does she order?

Leave your answer in terms of x and y.

_____

6

6.55 _____ 6.65

What number does the arrow point to?

_____

7

Headache tablets are sold in packets of 18.

How many complete packets can be made from 293 tablets?

_____

8

Which ratio is NOT the same as the ratio 12 : 60? Circle the letter.

A 6 : 30 **B** 2 : 10 **C** 1 : 5

D 5 : 1 **E** 24 : 120

9 1 8 9 15 16

Which is **neither** a square number **nor** a cube number? Circle the answer.

10

The Hundred Years War began in 1337 and finished in 1453. How long did it last?

_____

Total

Test time: 0   5   10 minutes

1

Stu was y years old 13 years ago.

How old will he be in 2 years time?

Leave your answer in terms of y.

_____

2

Key: = 10 loaves

= 5 loaves

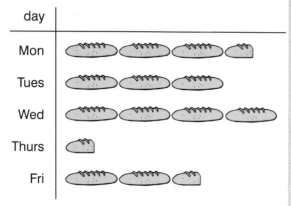

day	
Mon	
Tues	
Wed	
Thurs	
Fri	

The shop ran out of stock one day and had to shut early.

Which day do you think this occurred?

_____

3

There are 360 books in the school library.

$\frac{1}{5}$ of the books are fiction.

$\frac{2}{5}$ of the books are non-fiction.

The rest are reference books.

How many reference books are in the library?

_____

4

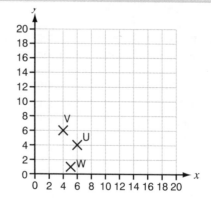

Look at the grid shown.

What are the coordinates of the points U, V and W?

Circle the answer.

A   U(6, 4)   V(4, 6)   W(5, 1)

B   U(4, 6)   V(6, 4)   W(1, 5)

C   U(3, 2)   V(2, 3)   W(2.5, 0.5)

D   U(6, 4)   V(4, 6)   W(4, 2)

E   U(6, 4)   V(4, 6)   W(6, 2)

5

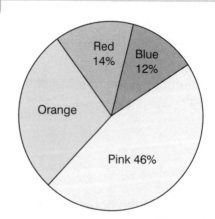

750 people were asked their favourite colour.

The results are displayed in the pie chart.

How many people liked orange?

_____

6

Year	Won	Drawn	Lost
2002	4	4	12
2003	6	6	8
2004	5	8	7

How many matches in total did the table tennis team not win?

_____

7

	18	
58	39	20
19	60	**?** 38

When every space is filled in, each row and each column adds up to 117.

Which number should replace the question mark?

_____

8

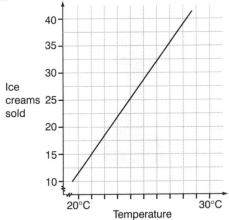

Temperature

The graph shows the number of ice creams sold depending on the temperature of the day. How many ice creams were sold when the temperature was 21°C?

_____

9

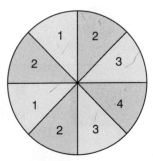

A game is shown above.

Players have to throw a dart at the board and whichever sector (wedge) the dart lands in is their score for that round.

The darts can not land on the borders.

All the throws of the darts are fair.

What is the probability of obtaining an odd number on the throw of the dart?

_____

10

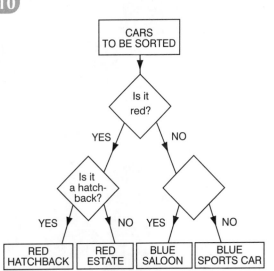

What is missing from the decision tree?

Circle the answer.

A Is it a sports car?

B IT IS A SPORTS CAR.

C Is it blue?

D IT IS BLUE.

E Is it a saloon?

Puzzle ①

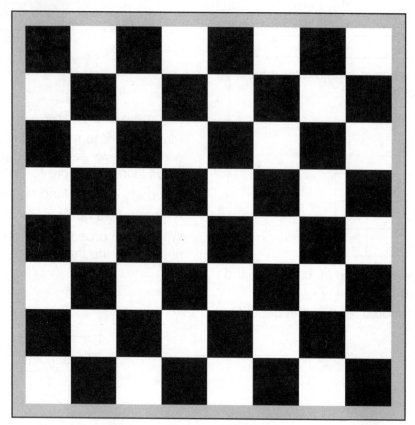

How many squares are on a chessboard? _____

Clues:

a How many different sized squares can you find? _____

b How many of the smallest squares can you find? _____

c How many of the other sizes of squares can you find? _____

Puzzle ❷

An office block has thirty offices numbered 1, 2, 3, up to 30.

Thirty caretakers work at the offices and they all flick the light switches before they leave at the end of the day.

They don't care whether the lights are on or off.
If the lights are on, they switch them off and if the lights are off they switch them on!

The first caretaker who leaves, switches every light off.

The second caretaker who leaves, flicks every second switch starting with office number two.

The third caretaker who leaves, flicks every third switch starting with office number three.

The fourth caretaker who leaves, flicks every fourth switch starting with office number four.

This continues until the thirtieth caretaker leaves and only flicks the switch in office number thirty.

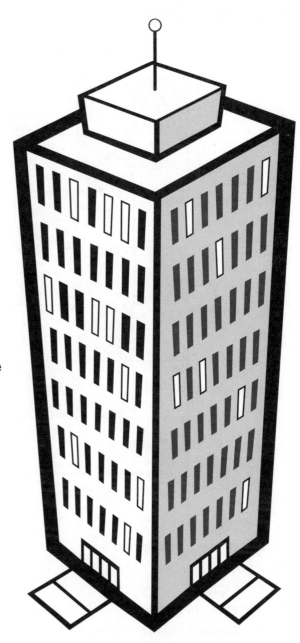

a Which offices are left with the lights off? _____

b What is special about these office numbers? _____

Puzzle ③

Complete the grid by answering the questions below.

	1	2		3	4	
5		6	7		8	9
10	11		12	13		
	14	15		16	17	
18		19	20		21	22
23	24		25	26		
	27			28		

Across

1 a dozen
3 half of one hundred and ten
6 a square number
8 three cubed
10 a multiple of thirteen
12 five squared plus six squared
14 six squared plus seven squared plus two
16 102 − 11
19 37 + 6
21 seven squared
23 two squared plus five squared
25 100 − 17
27 60 + 7
28 51 − 3

Down

2 a prime number
4 23 + 29
5 seven eights
7 a multiple of eleven
9 a number divisible by seven and eleven
11 79 − 21
13 a factor of nineteen
15 a multiple of thirty-seven
17 the number of pounds in a stone
18 double twenty-one
20 a multiple of nineteen
22 a multiple of twenty-three
24 two squared less than ten squared
26 divisible by seventeen

Puzzle ④

The numbers shown are the totals of the four numbers in that row or column.

Find the remaining totals and write them in the empty total boxes.

Puzzle ⑤

Five boxes each hold some one kilogram weights.
No two boxes weigh the same.

Their total weight is 31 kilograms.

It is possible to make any weight up to 31 kilograms using one or more boxes.

How much does each box weigh?

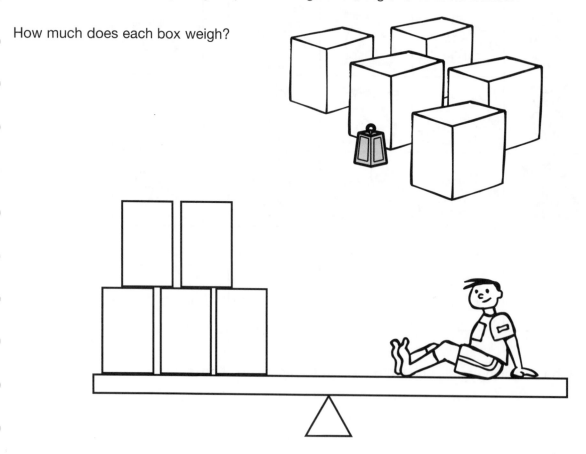

Progress Grid

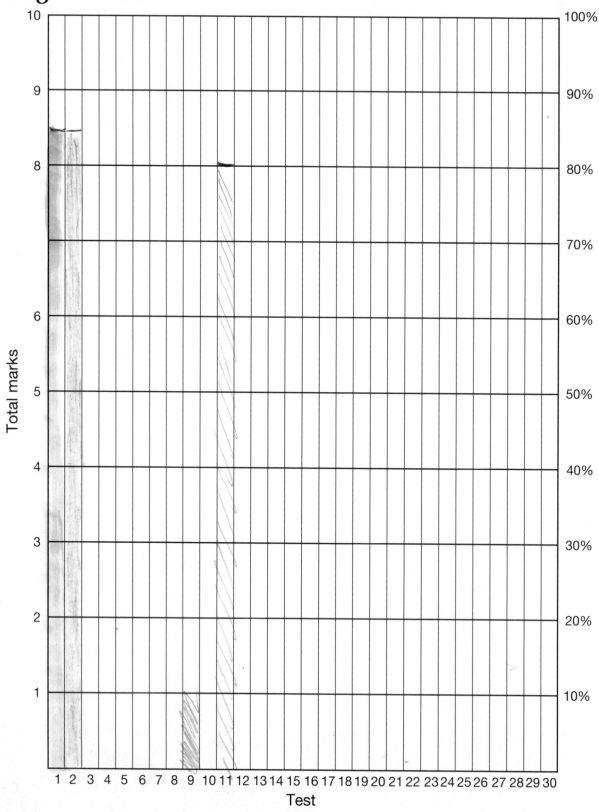